The
Hea
of
Sunday Worship

by
Colin Buchanan
Vicar of St. Mark's, Gillingham
Honorary Assistant Bishop in the Diocese of Rochester

GROVE BOOKS LIMITED
Bramcote   Nottingham   NG9 3DS

CONTENTS

Copyright Colin Buchanan 1992

FOREWORD

'We are constantly driven back to these Sunday activities. If they fail, there will be no church to tackle anything else. If they fail, where and how will men and women meet God? If they fail, the whole institution of the visible church will have failed.'

COB in *Patterns of Sunday Worship* (1972) page 4

THE COVER PICTURE

is by Peter Ashton

First Impression April 1992

ISSN 0144-1728

ISBN 1 85174 204 2

INTRODUCTION

Twenty years ago, in the first months of Grove Booklets on Ministry and Worship, I wrote a Booklet (no. 9 in the Series) entitled *Patterns of Sunday Worship*. The quotation in the Foreword on page 2 opposite comes from it. The booklet clearly met a need, setting out some principles for full-orbed worship on Sundays (including both word and sacrament). At the time the Parish Communion had spread far beyond a connoisseur few; evangelicals in particular were grappling with their own 1967 Keele resolution that 'we determine to work towards the practice of a weekly celebration of the sacrament as the central corporate service of the church'[1]; and the Church of England as a whole was about to wrestle with a new ethos of liturgy in the form of Series 3 communion (the immediate ancestor of Rite A). This rite not only brought the address to God into 'you' form, and thus crossed a cultural watershed, but it also gave far more responsibility to the local worship-leaders to use their creative discretion in the contents and presentation of the liturgy.

Patterns of Sunday Worship sold out fairly quickly, and, although it had been hastily put together, I took it to a second edition in 1975 with very little alteration. But when that next edition sold out, it was clear that a straight reprint would not do, and it is only now that the Series (and my own commitments) have allowed a new booklet to be written. This booklet then is the result of stopping the clock briefly in March 1992 to review the same issues. Times are moving faster now, and I would hardly today expect the seven-year currency that the two editions of the 1972 booklet gained. I would also hardly dare breathe today that the earlier booklet did not so much as mention the Charismatic Movement.

I make no apology for an element of hop-skip-and-jump introductory history. No individual, no congregation, no denomination, can understand itself or its own ways without a grasp of those influences which have formed it. A worship event composed of young and old alike, meeting together to worship with a sacred book nearly two thousand years old, and an order of worship not much younger, in a church building six hundred years old, singing hymns which are two hundred years old, led by a clergyman who is sixty years old, and using a liturgical text which is about twenty years old, whilst sitting on furniture which was replaced only last year, is inevitably the creation of the historical forces impacting upon it. So it is a critical appreciation of those historical forces which is needed for the church's understanding of itself at worship to-day.

Some of the impact of the twenty years since I last wrote on this subject on both the content and context of Christian worship in England is charted in the pages that follow. But of course the years have also had their impact on me, as I have had to engage with both the Christian revelation and the needs of the fast-changing times in many capacities—as University and College lecturer in Christian worship, as co-author and co-editor of liturgical texts on the Liturgical Commission and on General Synod, as leader of

[1] Philip Crowe (ed.) *Keele '67: The National Evangelical Anglican Congress Statement* (Falcon, 1967) p.35.

worship in College, parish, and a host of other circumstances, as father of a growing (and now grown up) family, as traveller round the Anglican Communion, participant in the International Anglican Liturgical Consultations, and secretary of the Group on liturgy at the 1988 Lambeth Conference, and latterly as incumbent of a parish. However, the most consistent and amazing stimulus over these years has come from the Group which has produced this unending Series of Booklets (and has had a big hand also in the companion Liturgical Studies and the monthly journal which I edit, *News of Liturgy*). I refer to the Group for Renewal of Worship (GROW), which I have been privileged to chair for twenty-one years. As a Group they may not be as well known as their booklets have become, though many members have now made their own deep mark upon official texts and reports of the Church of England and in a dozen other ways. But no-one could have looked (through various ups and downs of a public Christian life) for such sustained good humour, unfettered criticism, and marvellously creative thinking as I have found with these good friends. I imagine that readers of Grove Booklets throughout the world consider them friends also.

One major achievement of these twenty years has been to divert people's concern from a one-eyed concentration on authorized *texts*. It is much larger questions which have occupied me in this booklet. Similarly, I believe that virtually all sensible rationales for the establishment of the Church of England have disappeared in the same period, and we are now clearly a small-ish Church but *engaged in mission*.

One further thought that looking back over twenty years prompts is this: that a short booklet could not be definitive anyway—and doubly not so when both the times in which we live and my own mind are all on the move. I offer this to you as solely interim work.

1. WHAT IS OUR WORSHIP FOR?

There are various components of the public event we call 'worship'. It has been traditional in the Church of England to describe (and prescribe) the event as though it were wholly defined by its *text*. It is texts which are carefully trimmed and cautiously authorized within the Church of England—indeed it is at the level of texts that control is most easily exercised from the centre over the worship events of the local church. Many worshippers also think that the official texts they use are determinative of the event—and even argue for and against particular textual uses as though that were so. But it is not.

We are wise (for analysis and discussion purposes) to consider worship as not simply text but as a multi-faceted multi-dimensional *event*. Its categories of earthly components are as follows:
(a) The physical world—buildings, furnishings, ornamentation, musical instruments, books, robes, sacramental elements etc.

(b) The people—worship is a function of *people*, real people with faces, bodies, voices, relationships etc. (Traditional accounts which focussed on texts and textual programmes overlooked this.) Within the 'people' factor there are other skills and abilities laid under contribution, particularly those of leading.

(c) Time sequence—each regular event fits into a time rhythm, whether of the day, or the week, or the year, or (like marriage) the once-in-a-lifetime.

(d) The Christian story—within the event, for it to be Christian, the Christian story is repeated, by Bible reading, sermon, creed, prayer, praise, song, and in other ways.

The actual event on, say, a particular Sunday is a subtle combination of these components. A written liturgy is a kind of programme, and will probably take up (c) and (d) above. It is, however, very likely to take (a) for granted (though these physical components are different for every place of worship), and it has been traditional for Anglican accounts to ignore (b) almost entirely. The programme has been an up-front one which the clergy performed: full stop. It has been an all-consuming passion of the clergy, and has been generally assumed by the worshippers to be that kind of a clergy preserve (though the odd organist has at intervals established an alternative power-base . . .). But vitally worship is a function of *people*, and any number of well-oiled and well-prepared up-front programmes may still leave the people cold and uninvolved.

It is the concentration on those 'programmes' which has reinforced the importance of the liturgical texts in people's minds. This has been further buttressed by the necessity for 'authorizing' everything which is to be reckoned as 'liturgical text' (and sometimes rubric, which is itself textual), and declaring all variants substitutes illegal, whereas all other areas of worship, including hymnody, furnishings, sermons, leadership skills, etc.

etc. were totally uncontrolled, and dependent upon local and personal whim. Moreover, even within the programme itself, official texts take a much smaller part than Anglicans have usually bothered to stop and measure. A communion service of an hour will have only *ten minutes* of official text—and one of an hour and a half will also have but ten minutes. Something is going on in worship which traditional Anglican disputes have ignored.

So let us start this time with not the programme but the people. Why are the people 'going to church'?

I suppose that, at the Reformation time, the authorities who produced and enforced the reformed Book of Common Prayer were sure they were doing the country good, changing the hearts of the common people. The Acts of Uniformity were, at the point of enactment, concerned to ensure that scriptural truth became central to the diet of English people. The rules were, in a ruthless and paternalistic way, to do the people good. However, the principle of conformity quickly proved to operate the other way round. The monarchs began to sense that their own physical security, and that of the throne, rested upon the religious conformity of the country. And the people in turn began to sense that they were expected to conform uncritically in accordance with central policy, a policy which was serving the monarchy as much as the people.

If there was one distinguishing note of the Puritans of the sixteenth and seventeenth centuries it was that of nit-picking criticism. And the Puritans in turn reverted to the notion of an enforced diet which would do the people good—the diet being scripture, extempory prayer and strong sermons, rather than the liturgical exactnesses of the BCP, a use which was in the seventeenth century rarely accompanied by preaching, and perhaps even more rarely enhanced by it when it was.

So much for post-Reformation springs of action. In due course Toleration came, and the eighteenth century Church of England settled into a kind of torpor, in which the squire and his relations might make a minimal appearance on Sundays, but the peasants in the rural economy were marginalized from the church, and, if they were to catch any gospel at all, as like as not they would become new-fangled and 'enthusiastic' Methodists. Churchgoing in the parish churches very often ran on out of convention, with vast respectability, and (except in the few evangelical Anglican parishes) with an abhorrence of 'enthusiasm'.

In the nineteenth century, the working population moved in large numbers to the new industrial towns and knew little of the church there at all. The middle-classes on the other hand probably showed a greater propensity for churchgoing than in either the previous century or the following one. The Victorian Sunday was buttressed by the law. The growing interest in sport and entertainment was focussed on Saturday afternoons and evenings, and new conventions about doffing one's cap to God on Sundays arose. The Victorian father tended to ensure that his offspring took their place in worship week by week, and the habits became engrained. In the more exotic regions of the evangelical or anglo-catholic revivals there was also a strong sense of group solidarity—as in Northern Ireland to this day, it was important to the group identity that the turnout was good and was known to be good. It would be fair to say that in combination these factors built into the middle-classes at least a strong sense that it was their *duty* to be in church on Sundays, though whether the duty was traceable to God and his commands, or simply to human pressure over successive generations, it would be difficult to discern.

One common new element of Sunday worship in Victorian times was the weekly provision of communion. The general pattern from Tudor times till the nineteenth century was for communion to be celebrated in parish churches four times in the year, with Morning Prayer, Litany, and Ante-Communion (with or without sermon) as the staple morning diet on other Sundays.[1] Now weekly communion was restored—at 8 a.m. or thereabouts. It is said to have begun with Daniel Wilson, the evangelical vicar of Islington, who in the 1820s began a regular early morning service as a kind of overflow because his numbers were too great. It got taken up by the anglo-catholics, and it fitted well into their teaching of fasting communion. They would have tended to tell their people (from the mid-1850s onwards) that they had to be present at mass each week, though they would not necessarily expect to receive the elements each week (and in its extreme form such teaching would have required the worshipper to make his or her confession prior to receiving). Thus anglo-catholics moved into a Sunday pattern whereby the 'eight o' clock' was where people received communion, whereas a later mass might be the main morning service, but only the priest would then receive the elements. There was thus an 'obligation' (a good 'catholic' word.) to 'assist' (i.e. be present) at mass, but no obligation (beyond the three times a year in the BCP rubrics) to receive communion. Evangelicals and middle church people for their part settled down with an 'eight o' clock' for the particularly devout, and with Morning and Evening Prayer with sermons as the main diet of Sundays. Sermons were a very serious part of Sunday worship. There is reason to think that the gentry themselves went to the morning services, whilst their domestic staff in the morning prepared a substantial Sunday dinner, and then were duly sent to the slightly down-market evening service. Morning and evening alike offered hymns and sermons (and often anthems, as robed choirs spread across the land); neither morning nor evening offered the sacrament.[2]

[1] We can catch glimpses of the normality of such patterns by noting the reaction to John Wesley's move to have communion weekly, as part of the life of the 'Holy Club' (*sic*). He and his friends were promptly dubbed 'Methodists'—a title which remained into the post-1738 days of 'enthusiasm', though it was originally inspired by something nearer to rubricism. Eighteenth century church architecture also tells the tale—the buildings were 'auditory', square chambers with galleries for hearing (hearing the liturgy, that is, just as much as hearing sermons), and the communion tables went into a shallow apse or recess in the East wall, and were often almost entirely obscured by the central triple-decker pulpit in front of them.

[2] One curiosity in all this was the growing place of confirmation in the second half of the nineteenth century. Clearly confirmation was being treated as admission to communion. It was never till within living memory administered at a communion service—no, it came mid-week, and was followed a well-placarded 'First Communion' the following Sunday, usually at the eight o'clock. To take one person whose public role is known, Winston Churchill, who was confirmed at Harrow School in the 1880s, says that he
[continued overleaf

Had you asked the non-sacramentalist Victorian Sunday morning church-attender why he or she went, the answer might have been one of two sorts—the 'push' and the 'pull'.

'Push' is the character of *duty*. You *ought* to be there. There is either a command, or at least an unbreakable convention, which drives you there, irrespective of how much you like it, or what benefit you receive. We have seen the place that 'duty' had in anglo-catholicism—the teaching would be that the church required certain basic rules to be observed. Strong evangelicals would have sought their basis in scripture, and would come up with texts like 'they continued steadfastly in the apostles' doctrine and fellowship . . . ' (Acts 2.42) and 'not forsaking the assembling of your-selves together, as the manner of some is' (Hebrews 10.25). They would probably have added that we go to church to give as well to get, and that the great purpose of God in setting aside the sabbath day was to enable us to worship. They would certainly have dismissed a child's complaint that a particular preacher was boring as irrelevant to the issue. The people in the middle in the Church of England would have had a conventional sense of duty that said that God was there, and that we *knew* we *ought* to worship him, even if they were a bit uncertain about ultimate authorities or actual sanctions. Indeed, the non-churchgoer who apologized to the vicar for not attending was doing so from a vague irritating conscience which told her (or him) that God *was* there and we ought to be in worship regularly. 'Duty' still lurked around, even when people were in breach of it—and that phenomenon too endured to within living memory.

Was there then a 'pull'? Was there any identifiable *benefit* to be obtained from churchgoing? The anglo-catholics in the slum parts of the industrial cities claimed that exotic colour and ceremonial took people out of the squalor of their normal surroundings and offered them an alternative aesthetic experience (which was the gateway to entering the presence of God). Others would have said that superb music offered a parallel benefit. And others again would have cited powerful preaching as a great attrac-tion. Certainly, the advent of advertising church services in the religious and daily papers must have had an element of 'offering attractions'—of benefit 'pull'—to tempt the undecided readers. There was something on offer.

People who become creatures of habit are often unable to distinguish between 'push' and 'pull'. A habit does both to us at once, and we cheerfully—and perhaps even mindlessly—submit to both at once unreflectively. But if you deprive a creature of habit of that habit by sheer force or necessity, then you will encounter either a very unhappy person or a very released one. Then may be the time to enquire whether the force was behind the habit pushing or before the habit pulling.

continued from note 2 on page 7/
received communion once and then never again. Confirmation gained exalted status as a kind of puberty religious rite, but actually did not connect well to sacramental practice, largely because the jump into being a 'devout' weekly communicant at 8 a.m. on Sun-days was too great for the average 12-year-old. The exception would be where the parents themselves went at 8 a.m. regularly. Otherwise the pattern was set up for con-firmation to be the church's leaving certificate, as it was still reputed to be in my younger days.

But all the Victorian ways we have noted (and this would be broadly true in the Free Churches also) depended upon a widespread prior knowledge that God, even the God of the Bible, was *there*. This presupposition lasted in all parts of English society far into the twentieth century, but has now largely departed. The man-in-the-street is not now a Christian who happened not to go to church last Sunday. And so church worship in turn is that of a small, gathered, and somewhat committed, community with distinctive group agenda, and not a kind of general activity of a vaguely Christian population, any or all of whom might be present on occasion.

2. TWENTIETH CENTURY DEVELOPMENTS

A time-traveller going back to the beginning of the twentieth century would find high and low alike in the Church of England very formal, very clericalist, and very predictable—even if between two adjacent parishes a transition from high to low or low to high would produce trans-cultural shock. We have seen that in neither would word and sacrament come together; and we could add that in neither of them would children have any place in main worship, save that of silent small adults.

Whilst the First World War shook up many traditions, it was not until December 1927 that the Parish Communion as we know it today came to birth. At St. John's, Newcastle-upon-Tyne, in the words of Henry de Candole, 'we transformed a 10 o'clock Children's Eucharist without communicants into a Parish Eucharist, then and ever since habitually known as the "9.15"'.[1] The time was, no doubt, dictated by the anglo-catholic requirement of receiving communion fasting—not all 'party' features departed overnight—but the upshot was to bring parents and children together, to bring word and sacrament together, and to form, from pastoral motives, a rite which was intended to lie at the heart of parish life.

In the 1930s this Sunday pattern widened into many parishes. It gained theological reinforcement from growing awareness of the continental Liturgical Movement, in which the over-formal inherited Roman uses were under criticism for their lack of authenticity, intelligibility, and pastoral sensitivity. The rites were not enabling an unclouded vision of the Lord, nor enabling the church to be or to be seen to be the church. So, as the seeds of Vatican II were being sown on the continent, some of the positive and practical side of the protest came into the Church of England.[2] The simple appeal of it was expressed in the slogan 'The Lord's Service for the Lord's People on the Lord's Day'.

I think it is true to say that this is the *only* major development of the twentieth century in the pattern of Sunday worship. The Church of England has become irreversibly sacramentalist. And it is right that it should be so. The Lord told his followers 'Do this in remembrance of me'. We, looking at the Bible, might have argued in an academic way that the annual passover supper was now to become an annual Christ-commemoration supper. But the disciples obviously did not see this as an option. They shared meals

[1] Henry de Candole 'Twenty-five years on' in D. M. Paton (ed.) *The Parish Communion To-Day* (SPCK, London, 1962) pp.1-2. The actual month is interesting—it is arguable that more far-reaching liturgical history was being made quite without publicity on Tyneside than anything happening on Thamesside amidst the trumpets and alarms at the defeat in the Commons of the proposed 1927 Prayer Book a few days later.
[2] The books which gave this reinforcement were: Gabriel Hebert, *Liturgy and Society* (Faber, 1935, reprinted as a Faber paperback, 1961); Gabriel Hebert (ed.), *The Parish Communion* (SPCK, 1937); Bro. Edward, *Sunday Morning—The New Way* (SPCK, 1938). It is worth noting that the Roman Catholic Liturgical Movement broke surface in a somewhat academic format, with conferences, books and journals long preceding any official changes, whilst in the Church of England a purely practical step was taken in parish after parish and it only acquired intellectual support as it went along. But it might well have been a true instinct.

with their Lord in his resurrection (with a strong sacramental overtone in 'he was made known to them in the breaking of the bread'); they broke bread from house to house daily after the liberating power of the Spirit came on them at Pentecost; and they met naturally on 'the first day of the week to break bread' (Acts 20.7). Whilst there is no absolute command in the New Testament to 'do this *once a week*', it is clear that the church did meet on the first day of the week, and did 'do this'. And in the post-apostolic era, when persecution came, the one activity which remained the distinctive mark of being Christian was meeting together once a week for this meal. This they would not surrender, even though they might be imprisoned or put to death.

Alongside this change in the *pattern* of Sunday worship, there has also come about a change of *style* as *ethos.* In essence, worship has become less formal, or rather less formalistic. Liturgy has been allowed to have a human face, and rubricism has faded accordingly. New styles of singing have arisen—whether charismatic choruses, or Taizé chants, or Grail style cantor and antiphon. New forms of congregational participation have emerged also—not only in the new roles of laypersons in reading (or dramatizing) the Scriptures, but also in their leading the prayers, contributing various gifts, or chrisms, in 'open' periods during worship, in laying on of hands with prayer for healing and in distributing the elements.[1]

Of course, the last twenty years have also seen the coming of new *texts.* These have also changed our worship events considerably. My only plea is that we should not treat new texts as the be-all and end all of our worship changes. They have their own fascination. There are exciting new texts to come before General Synod in the next year or two. But they are *not* the theme of this booklet. The heart of Sunday worship is to be sought elsewhere.

---

[1] A natural further development has been the use of laypersons to take the elements from a celebration to people who are sick or shut in, often with quite a satellite liturgy and pastoral encouragement as part of the visit.

3. EVANGELICAL OBJECTIONS

Though the Parish Communion advocates for the first forty years or so argued that they were bringing together high and low, it is clear that this was whistling to keep their own courage up. The change to a Parish Communion was almost invariably made in middle-to-high parishes. Evangelicals not only did not follow the trend—they actively opposed it. It is worth noting the grounds of their objections.

In its pre-1970 form the Parish Communion presented the following problems:

Firstly, it appeared to treat 'being in communion' as a panacea for all spiritual ills (and thus as a covert surrender to anglo-catholicism); the prevalent evangelical view would have been rather to see it as a kind of spiritual treat, to be used sparingly—topping up the spiritual diet rather than being a basic ingredient of it.

Secondly, it was viewed as being offputting to newcomers. Whilst a broad 'fringe' persists around the life of the church, then, it was argued, fringe people can find their way into worship more easily with a non-sacramental service than with a communion, which inevitably excludes them—and evangelicals greatly disliked the whole principle of unbelievers being present at communion, even as non-communicants.

Thirdly, the Parish Communion saw a diminishing of preaching, on which of course evangelicals placed great weight. It was true that until the 1970s the greater the number of communicants, then the greater the number of persons to whom a presbyter—often single-handed—had to minister, and the longer he would take in doing so. If the whole service was to be kept within bounds (Anglicans generally have had very fierce time-limits upon their endurance of church services), then time had to be pruned elsewhere—and the only obvious candidate was the sermon. If young children were present that also put constraints upon the time taken for preaching. And the tendency was for the sermon to go down to a seven-minute 'liturgical homily'—tidy, churchy, related to the theme of the Sunday, very often related to receiving communion, quite probably poker-faced, passionless and powerless—so at least it seemed to the sermon-centred evangelicals.

Fourthly, the very slogan 'The Lord's Service for the Lord's People on the Lord's Day' pushed all the 'oncers' towards the morning—and the Parish Communion quickly undermined the evening service in the parishes where it was introduced. Of course the 1960s and 1970s saw a great decline in 'twicers' anyway, but many who had previously gone in the evenings only now moved to the morning. And many a parish which felt fairly alive on Sunday mornings felt fairly dead on Sunday evenings. But this was an appalling prospect to be asked to embrace in many evangelical parishes. Sunday evenings were a focus for young people, and after-church activities had a place almost as important as church ones. If evening church ceased or became thin, a colossal loss of committed young people seemed likely to follow.

Family Services

Instead, evangelicals have tended since 1960 to develop a different pattern. Its most characteristic feature is the 'Family Service'—a non-sacramental, loosely structured, event with enormous variations. At one end of the liturgical spectrum it is a simplified Matins—at the other it is a kind of party. It is intended always to be easy for new families to enter, to make people at ease in crossing the church threshhold (certainly a difficult step for some), and to be relatively undemanding in its length, character and contents.[1]

The Family Service fits into parish strategies in different ways. In some it is *the* central service of each Sunday morning—a pattern found most often in new housing areas, and pioneer mission churches. In others it is a once-a-month phenomenon, bringing together families which are on other Sundays scattered, the children being in teaching groups of various ages, whilst parents may indeed be at communion, or may only come to church when there is a family service. Occasionally a family service precedes or follows some other 'main service', either because overflowing numbers require two shifts, or because an old-fashioned Matins congregation would not accept change, but has clung to its rights, and a new pattern has been started alongside it.

Evangelical Sacramentalism?

Certainly too communion has become much more important to evangelicals since the early 1960s. They have shed much of the anti-sacramentalism which represented their fear-ful reaction to the false (as they saw it) sacramentalism of the anglo-catholic movement. Communion services as the main Sunday morning or evening worship at intervals are now almost invariable—sometimes once a month in the morning, once a month in the evening; sometimes alternating between morning and evening on a week- and-week-about basis.

An advocate of a basic rhythm of weekly communion must offer some critique of these patterns. The issue with family services is how the worshippers are to be moved on into both adult teaching and communion—how indeed the principle of weekly communion can be combined with it. The issue with once a month in the morning, once a month in the evening, or the week-and-week-about pattern, is that there is no rhythm for the individual at all. Indeed many will sit in church and say to themselves as the service starts 'Oh, it's communion this morning'. That is to treat the communion not as central, but as an interesting variant on non-sacramental services. There is no evidence anywhere of worshippers being either taught or expected to alternate between morning and evening themselves in order to be in communion, and the only people who

---

[1] There has been a growing concern in the Church of England to provide liturgical resources for such services. The first major move in this direction came from Michael Botting and the Church Pastoral-Aid Society in the 1960s. As the official services moved into addressing God as 'you', so the unofficial materials moved also. A further major step forward was Michael Perry's *Church Family Worship* (Hodder and Stoughton, 1986). Official liturgy is now also in prospect, as *Patterns for Worship* (CHP, 1989) contains a great range of innovative Bible-based responsive and participatory resources—though, at the time of writing, the House of Bishops is proving fairly cautious in respect of these.

would become weekly communicants through this pattern would be the consistent 'twicers'. People become communicant by accident, rather than design.

Furthermore, if it is alleged that to have a regular spread of non-sacramental services because they are easier for outsiders, then we would need to know that outsiders know when it is *not* to be communion and deliberately choose those occasions to come to church. Experience runs contrary to this—that where people do drift in occasionally to church, they do so for random personal, private, or family reasons, which are rarely if ever related to prior knowledge of whether it is a sacramental or non-sacramental service they are entering. And whether or not they feel comfortable or at ease depends upon the kind of welcome they receive, the user-friendliness of whatever is put in their hands (or on a screen), and the sheer helpfulness of the persons they sit beside, much more than upon the actual order or contents of the rite itself. In many parts of the country we should reckon that outsiders nowadays find prayers and Bible-reading and hymns as strange as they do communion, and there is no reason why such persons, if they visit a church service, should not find Christians undertaking the whole of the distinctive Christian agenda.

At the same time, another objection listed in the pre-1970 set above has diminished to vanishing point. In 1970 there came about Convocation Regulations which allow lay persons of either sex to be nominated to the bishop to distribute both elements. Such persons do not have to be licensed Readers, and it is obvious sense both to have good numbers of them, and to use several places in the building for the distribution of communion rather than to have an unnecessary lengthening of the time taken. Thus the ministry of the word should not be squeezed by this factor, and usually nowadays is not.

These lines of reply do not of themselves solve problems of evening services—or of the kinds of people who most naturally gravitate to an evening service. They are the subject of further treatment in chapter 5 below.

14

4. BUILDING UP THE PEOPLE FOR MISSION

In *Patterns of Sunday Worship* twenty years ago, I wrote about communion as follows:

'. . . no other pattern of the main service of Sunday will serve us well in the future. That future may be far, or very near. But the moment the gulf between church and society reaches a certain width, then the uncommitted fringe will start to disappear, and the church will need to stand up and be counted. The non-sacramental services do not, and could not, achieve this end. They have no sanctions attached, and remain in their very nature services which individuals choose to attend or not as their disposition takes them. And if the sermon is the central drawing feature of these services, then it is only a matter of time before individuals start to discover they can get just as good sermons on TV or even through a cassette service. It is exactly the difference between the Bible and other books. Other books may be helpful and interesting, and they may be so in a variety of ways to different persons. But no-one can ever be told that it is part of his duty towards God to read this book or that. *That* is only true of the Bible. So it is with services. Many may be helpful, but only communion has the command of God behind it. . . . (evangelicals) have tended by their practice to lump holy communion into the same category of services one attends if it is found helpful . . . '[1]

We should now make no mistake: the times have changed, and the scenario anticipated above is upon us.

Firstly, we now reckon on little over 2% of the nation being in Church of England worship events with any regularity on Sundays. That 2% is a national figure, an aggregate which provides simply an average against which each parish can measure itself. The actual figure will vary enormously and local congregations should neither be discouraged by less than 2% nor over-encouraged by more—for obviously inner urban parishes, which may be 90% Moslem and perhaps for the rest largely Roman Catholic, are going to have a low showing: and by definition the average is kept at 2% by the fact that some parishes are well above it.

We are thus numerically extremely weak in living worshippers. And if we took sub-divisions by age and by sex we would find that, for instance, our men between 18 and 38 years of age were way down to more like .2% or even .02% of the national population in that age category. So we are almost at the point where, despite our buildings standing around the land, and our notable cathedrals and other institutions, the angels would need not just powerful telescopes, but spy-in-the-sky latest technology, actually to detect our people going to worship on Sundays. Any of us of course who are in a parish of 10,000 may kid ourselves that 72 people—or 127 people—going through the doors on a Sunday represents strength, but this is simply by comparison with two years ago when, say, the figures were 59 and 92. By comparison with the vast millions of the

---

[1] COB, *Patterns of Sunday Worship*, p.9.

nation we are a tiny handful. But the relevance at this moment is that, if we are so few, then what we do when we *do* meet is crucial. For clearly we are engaged in mission.

I want to hold on to that word 'meet'. Liturgy is the distinctive activity of Christians when they *meet*. In the New Testament they did not refer to 'holding a church service', but instead they simply said 'When the disciples came together' (Acts 20.7) or 'When you come together, it is not to eat the Lord's Supper' (1 Cor. 11.17). They came together, and, as far as we can see, they did their church business (what we would call PCC business) at the same time as singing psalms and saying prayers and exhorting and sharing the sacramental bread and wine. And this all occurred within the context of a larger meal. Their own description was 'coming together'—but in our terms they clearly *met*.

Perspectives for a Decade of Evangelism

We have to set this today in the context of a call to evangelism. There used, of course, to be guest services—and in some areas where there is a genuine fringe there may still be a case for them. Sometimes there is a variant, as, for instance, when all people who have been married in a particular parish are invited back to a special rite of renewing marriage vows. These are inevitably rare and 'once off'. And the threshhold role of regular 'family services' has been discussed above.

In general, I suspect, we have passed the time, at least in urban priority areas, when we can expect good numbers of people 'out there' to be a kind of penumbra, just waiting to be invited to church. Evangelism means outreach—we ask God to 'send us *out*'. We are going to where the people are. This in turn has various implications.

(a)   The agenda when we meet must be agenda for the faithful, securing them in the faith and equipping them for this 'going out'. Church life is not to be distorted all the time by being planned centrally for unbelievers, in the faint hope that they may yet show up.

(b)   We must, however, qualify that by urging people to keep an eye open for the stray outsider. There is such a person in 1 Corinthians 14, and when he drifts into a Christian assembly what he encounters makes him fall down and say 'Surely God is among you?'. I know such people exist to-day, as at intervals I find myself confirming them: and what happened when they first showed their noses in church—often to their own surprise—has been vital in their conversion.[1] I strongly suspect that the human warmth with which people were received will be as important as the programme being followed. And we should not make our worship events too culturally difficult for newcomers—we have an offence of the cross confronting them as it is, and we should not add an offence of the culture.

[1] I should perhaps further add that Paul expects this response from a man who walks into an assembly where prophecy is being used (1 Cor.14.24-25), and Paul's point is that he will understand what is going on. The opposite case is where people speak in strange languages, which, to paraphrase St. Paul, will be like double dutch to outsiders. So we set up our programme for the insiders, but not without a concern for the stray enquirer who finds himself or herself present at our worship. We certainly have to watch our *culture*, lest it is 'speaking in strange languages' to the outsider.

(c) Perhaps I might push this argument a stage further. I believe that the secularizing times themselves will force a more sacramental stance upon unsacramental believers. For what the eucharist does is to bring the individual to the point of commitment, to taking sides for Jesus Christ, and so to enable the church corporately then to stand up and be counted. And that, the semi-public identifying of the church and of its active members, is the base-line for outgoing evangelism.

And if we are to be sacramentally bounded and sustained, then I suggest two further implications which must be weighed:

(i) we must be careful about our administration of infant baptism.[1]

(ii) the proper concomitant of this is infant and child communion. Whilst there may be problems about the limits of who should be admissible, we must surely reckon for our own children that they are to be brought up as one with us in the body of Christ from the start (i.e. from the point of baptism), not only for scriptural and doctrinal reasons, but also for the practical and pastoral purpose that they should be sustained as believers from the start, and should be united with their parents at the Lord's Table right from the start.[2]

Examining the Agenda

So in the 1990s what are the people of God to do when they meet? An hour, an hour and a half, perhaps even two hours, are seized from busy weeks.[3] The church meets. What will it now *do*? And what will it do so that it does not simply maintain its existing members in a state of stupefied religious semi-consciousness, preparing ultimately to bury each other as the years pass by? What will it do instead to enable it to build itself up and propagate the faith of Jesus Christ in the neighbourhood? Here the question goes far beyond the particular liturgical tastes of this or that group, or the preaching abilities of this or that vicar, or the ceremonial accoutrements of this or that party. Let it be that the people are going to join together in the eucharist, and are going to stand up and be counted as the Lord's people at that same eucharist, how, then, are they to do it?

[1] I have of course an axe to grind here. I am president of the Movement for the Reform of Infant Baptism (MORIB), and I want the credibility of baptism to be sustained, with a true enrolling of the candidate into God's missionary task-force, the church. See the Grove Books list of materials on initiation (including my *Policies for Infant Baptism*, no. 98 in this Grove Worship Series), or write to MORIB, c/o The Vicarage, Clifton-on-Teme, Worcestershire.

[2] I was a member of the Knaresborough working party from 1982 to 1985, and drafted quite a bit of its report, *Communion before Confirmation?* (Church Information Office, 1985). I was also a member of the Boston International Anglican Liturgical Consultation in 1985 which made a substantial Statement on the subject, *Children and Communion*. I wrote *Children in Communion* (no. 112 in this Grove Series) in 1990, and shared also in the Toronto Fourth International Anglican Liturgical Consultation in 1991, the Statement from which, 'Walk in Newness of Life', is published as no. 118 in this Series, i.e., David Holeton (ed.) *Christian Initiation in the Anglican Communion* (1991). Sadly, at the time of writing there exists no pressure group (comparable to MORIB, say) to seek this change.

[3] I recognize that Sunday itself is not available to all sorts of people nowadays. See Appendix 1 on page 24 below.

We could do worse than go back to that original picture of the church on the evening of the day of Pentecost.

(a) The believers *met*. They met in each others' homes; they met to learn the apostles' teaching and to engage in prayers; they met to break bread; and they met to support each other.

Traditional Anglicanism has rarely had this character to a main Sunday service. Indeed you were almost promised in the past that you could sneak in anonymously, meet no-one, and sneak out without having to love anybody. 'Worship' was private, relating the believer to God, and doing so in physical juxtaposition to others who were following the same private agenda, but not expecting them to relate to each other.

Yet this 'received' pattern is quite foreign to the intrinsic nature of communion as we find it in the New Testament. It is clearly far removed from both the social character of the shared meals of Acts 2.42-47, let alone the direct command of the Lord at the Last Supper to love one another. However, it has been possible and usual for a worshipper at an Anglican rite to evade the whole challenge of those scriptures, and to remain in secure formal isolation. And now, what the 'common loaf' did not achieve the Kiss of Peace has modestly begun. Your neighbour faces you—and she has a face, and her face looks you in the eye, and even before the two of you grasp hands, you are both having to acknowledge each other through your eye-contact as real people invading each others' lives, however briefly, as part of God's building up of Christ's body. The eucharistic prayer and administration which follow may be fairly formal, but the inroads have already begun. The meal is irretrievably corporate.

(b) But suppose there is no other meeting. Suppose our programme still gives out a message that people may come as atomized individuals, may hide from each other, and may be relieved if they get home without being button-holed by anybody; suppose it tells them that they will not have to do anything which exposes them as different from anyone else. Then slowly, slowly, Anglicans do begin to wake up to the fact that at the main meeting of the church on Sunday people do not actually meet. The general response has been to create other events called 'meetings' to help them meet.[1] But that still dodged the issue of whether or not the central meeting of the week should not itself be a *meeting*. It is by *meeting* others that people discover themselves: it is by relating to others that people find supportive fellowship: and it is as the naturally unlike meet each other, *because they are in Christ together,* that a supernatural fellowship is built up, manifesting a loving community to the world.

[1] Once upon a time it was parish breakfasts after communion. Then, as parish communions got later in the morning (because the Pope had relaxed the fasting rule), it became coffee after the main morning service. In many parishes there are home meetings or other midweek instruction or worship events during the week, but the 2% on Sundays regularly go down to less than a quarter of that for mid-week meetings. And at mid-week events we are simply flanking the central meeting, not re-working it.

(c)   I need hardly add that the traditional Anglican fare left the laypeople speechless. People have been busily not drawing attention to themselves and the leaders would never put the spotlight on them. The back row is apparently perfectly safe in church, and large numbers, to avoid being exposed, to avoid embarrassment, are traditionally heading for those back rows.[1] But we are trying to develop people as people. We want them to be more confident and mature than simply those who sing hymns and say responses as members of an unthinking drill-squad.

We have an evangelistic mission which is upon us, and preachers are quite likely to urge their hearers to witness for Jesus Christ when they are out in the world. And so they should. Yet we omit a crucial stage, which should be happening *in worship.* For we are asking worshippers to speak for Jesus Christ in unsympathetic contexts *when we never give them a chance to say anything about him in sympathetic ones.* Surely along with our sacramentalism 'along with our monologue preaching, along with psalms and hymns and prayers and confessions—let alone robes and processions and pomp and ceremonial—we should be *training* the laity, and building them up? And my point is simply that each one needs to hear himself or herself speak something to God or about God in the presence of others— something, that is, which is from that individual himself or herself. It may be a contribution in group Bible Study, it may be a contribution in informal prayer, it may be testimony, it may be no more initially than mentioning the name of a sick person in the context of an open slot in the liturgical intercessions. It is, I submit, one great outcome of the Charismatic Movement that all the worshippers have been treated as in principle having a contribution to make—a gift *(charisma)* to bring. This is exactly what is found in the scriptures (see 1 Cor. 14.26, for instance), and if truly implemented means that the people are becoming confident in speaking of God and of the things of God, and to God, in the presence of each other. Indeed they are in a true sense addressing each other.[2] *Then* they may be able to address the world outside.

It is not only our traditional formal liturgical programme which has made it difficult for the individual to contribute personally and unembarrassedly, it is also the fixed character of our church interiors. But against these pressures how, within our Sunday programme, are our people not just to survive, but to be built up and to be humbly articulate in the faith? Is it so far distant from conventional Anglicanism to

---

[1] The cumulative effect of most people trying to sit near the back is pretty grim. There is a variant on this, where everybody who arrives early sits at the end of the row, guarding it against all-comers. This provides a totally unwelcoming vista—the late-comer has to push past someone to get into a seat, and the sense of at least marginal mutual resentment is built into that embarrassment.

[2] If this sounds like too great a departure from worshipping God, may I refer you to a discussion of this on pp.20-21 below. It is notable that in Eph. 5.19-20 Paul says in effect that we are *simultaneously* addressing each other and giving praise to God, and there is a definition around that worship is addressing God in the presence of each other and each other in the presence of God. It is interestingly reinforced by a fuller combing of the New Testament in I. Howard Marshall 'How did the early Christians *worship* God?' in *Churchman* Vol. 99 no. 3 (1985).

arrange small prayer-groups or Bible-study groups, or simply buzz-groups within the main Sunday worship event that we cannot do it? Or should we be working at all-age education (with all-age worship) in such a way as to help all our members to become articulate?[1] Or should we put our trust more heavily in mid-week 'meetings' or once-a-quarter whole day conferences, or what? Remember, we are trying to train a people of God to reclaim the world.

Speechlessness of course often reflects cluelessness.[2] For we have an accompanying endemic problem in our inherited Sunday patterns—it is not at all clear that people are learning the faith from our teaching pro-grammes. This is not simply a question of whether we preach for ten minutes or twenty. (Though I prefer twenty, I fully concede that the attention-span does not easily stretch beyond the ten—and I have a nasty suspicion that, for all the thousands of preparation-hours and delivery-hours that have gone into sermons which I have heard, yet the residuum left with me would hardly appear to justify it all—and I write as one who himself preaches . . .). No, my point is that monologue preaching is not only running a risk of leaving little deposit behind when it is gone, but also that we have no means of monitoring what is learnt—if anything is. The church of God has run on into a modern age with an ancient form of com-munication, and although we may work hard at making it work, we still tend to concentrate on the question 'What do we teach?' rather than the acid test 'What are the people of God *learning*?'

Objections

I can hear the criticism rising (because I have heard it in conferences and lectures, and now know its character). The objection takes the form: 'You want a matey togetherness, talking to each other, sitting in a circle perhaps, and worrying about what people are *learning*, when the real object of our worship-event is *worship*.' It is expressed thus by Aidan Kavanagh:

'Some signs of this . . . are the tendency . . . to produce the approved sort of community which celebrates middle-class values of joining, meeting and "speaking out"; to use these two endeavours as means to "create community" . . . to move away from the art of ceremony and symbol towards verbalization as the assembly's main medium of communication within itself . . . the liturgy becomes perceived by

---

[1] Some hints of ways of creating these radical new patterns are to be found in other Grove Booklets, including Judith Rose *All-Age Education on Sundays* (Pastoral Series no. 11), and Trevor Lloyd *Introducing Liturgical Change* (Worship Series no. 87)—and there is more in prospect.

[2] The classic Anglican confession of faith is 'Vicar, I know what I believe, but I cannot say it'. A more rigorous analysis might be that the speaker does *not* know what he or she believes. The clergy often connive at this, by saying 'Some things are too deep for words' and such-like apologias. I find that extraordinary—we have church services which are virtually words end-to-end, an hour or more *crowded* with words to and about God—and then, as soon as people are out of the building, the faith is too profound to be encap-sulated in mere words. Yet God is revealed by word, it was the Word who became flesh, it is the word with which we are put in trust, and the word of God is good *news* for the world. If we cannot say it, it is almost certainly not because it is too profound for us, but because we are vague and foggy and ignorant about its contents and unpractised at expressing it informally. And thus we have no message for the world around us.

many as less an obedient standing in the alarming presence of the living God in Christ than a tiresome dialectical effort at raising the consciousness of middle-class groups concerning ideologically approved ends and means.'[1]

I quote this extract in order to confront it. The point at issue is a simple one: was the New Testament Christian community one which gave high value to 'joining, meeting and "speaking out" ' and to 'verbalization'? It is an easy task to establish that these activities were very close to the heart of the New Testament community, and thus that they are not only not to be despised by the church to-day but are to be used to build up the people of God. We add that they are in no way characteristically and exclusively 'middle-class values'—rather they are Christian and community tools, and this could be illustrated in many modern Christian congregations all over the earth, and by no means especially in middle-class ones.

Perhaps I could slip in a little of the substance of 1 Corinthians 14. I am not staying on the issue Paul is handling, as to which of the two functions in competition at Corinth—i.e. vernacular prophecy and unknown languages—gives the better result or has a higher value with God. Paul's argument is well known. Instead I cite the points on which Paul assumes his readers would all naturally agree with him and accept his principles.

Firstly, there are going to be various people addressing the assembly—and their number has in his time to be curbed rather than stimulated (14.24-32). They are not giving 'set-piece' contributions but are speaking either from some word they have brought individually, or else from the spur of the moment.[2]

Secondly, they are to address *each other*. The great criterion by which Paul assesses their contributions is whether they speak to each other for 'strengthening, encouragement and comfort' (14.3). The same principle is true of what is in formal grammatical terms addressed to God—i.e. prayer and thanksgiving—as when I give thanks my neighbour must be able to say 'amen' (14.16). Indeed when he can say 'amen', then he is being 'edified' or built up (14.17). The words I use touch him, gather him up into the prayer I am uttering, enable him to say 'amen' and in the process build him up. The same possibility is built into unknown languages, *so long as someone translates into the vernacular* (14.5, 28, etc.). Anything which God alone can understand, but which is not transparent to the assembly, is of no use except to the speaker (14.2,4).

Thirdly, they are to *hear* each other, for they are to 'weigh' what is said (14.29). They are engaged in a fascinating assembly-wide conversation (along with prayer and thanksgiving which are also corporate) in the presence of God, and that is how God manifests himself to them. Indeed, 'verbalization' seems to be the keynote—the only question is 'how?', and

[1] A. Kavanagh 'Liturgical Inculturation: Looking to the Future' in *Studia Liturgica* 20 (1990), p.98 (Quoted by W. Jardine Grisbrooke in *Liturgy* (Vol. 16, no. 4, 1992) p.22.
[2] Ideally, I suspect, they would be responding to each others' words—which is how the word of Christ is to 'dwell in them *richly*' (Col. 3.17—where it is clearly also *corporately*).

there is no question about 'whether?'.[1] It is at this point that the Charismatic Movement has made its most significant inroad into traditional Anglican patterns of worship. There should be no more difficulty in contributing in worship than there is at a business meeting. And, of course, modern authorized and proposed rites do give space and encouragement to this, and we ought to be working on it, to help build the people up.[2] For thus they can become unembarrassedly articulate about Christ. It is of course very hard for people to address other in large buildings where the congregation sits in straight rows facing in one direction. It feels artificial to ask people to come to the front to use a microphone. Yet in most buildings 200 people can easily hear each other if they are 'in the round' (or 'the oval' or whatever).

So is this mere mateyness, with no sense of transcendence? Do we have to face in one direction and only do drill-squad activities to have a sense of God's greatness? I do not believe this for a moment, and I note again that it is in 1 Corinthians 14, where mutual address is being advocated so strongly by Paul, that he also anticipates that a newcomer entering even by accident will *fall down* and say 'Surely God is among you?'.

The Overall Strategy
What is the place of the communion rite at the heart of all this? Well, the meal is the place of meeting. Of course it involves meeting with God, but it is the people of God meeting with him as they meet with each other. As in the days before Constantine there is no substitute. It is eating together which bonds us.

This is not simply a place of refuge, a place of being quiet and still whilst withdrawn briefly from a busy and secular world. This is the place where the church of God identifies itself ('stands up and is counted'), and girds itself for its mission in the world. Without the communion there is no identifiable body of Christ to be his presence in the world. Without the communion there is nothing from which we can be sent out into the world. Without the communion there is no testable Christian centre or point of focus to which enquirers in the world can be pointed, into which converts can be introduced through baptism. And without that eschatological feast which is communion, a feast of love and of the reign of God, we are modelling nothing about the transformation of society which is our larger task in mission. This is our deliverance from a privatized personal discipleship into marching in and with the people of God on the mission God has given them. This is our glimpse of glory together, a glimpse which itself stirs us in our mission.

[1] The intriguing question to readers to-day should be not so much the nature of prophecy and unknown languages (though they inevitably have their interest), but the question of *who leads*. Paul gives no hint of anyone chairing or steering the assembly (unless it be in 1 Cor. 12.28, on which see my *Leading Worship*, no 76 in this Series, p.5). It is difficult to believe that there was no-one chairing the assembly then, and that we need no-one in this role to-day (though the Brethren movement, and perhaps the Quaker movement, have functioned on that assumption).

[2] Is there post-apostolic precedent? Well, it looks as though contributions were fairly free in the Didache. More to the point, in Justin Martyr around 150 AD, the people stand up and *jointly* (*First Apology* 65.1 and 67.5) offer prayers and thanksgivings, and it looks like an extemporary prayer meeting within the eucharist. This extemporary feature of worship fades from the record as time goes on, but in the beginning it is strongly there.

5. SUNDAY EVENING

I wrote twenty years ago that teaching should be a leading component of Sunday evening worship. My main concern was that Sunday evenings should not be abandoned, however strong the pressures towards the centrality of Sunday mornings might be. There are various different categories of persons, including the lonely, the 'twicers', the shift workers, and many others, for whom such provision looks highly desirable. Sunday evening is in many places a young people's time also, and after-church activities also may be important to them. If there are persons who can rarely or never join in the main Sunday morning communion, then a regular (perhaps monthly) communion should be part of the evening provision. And there may well be places where Sunday evening activities could well be re-started with home groups.

Yet there has grown an element which I did not properly anticipate twenty years ago—'Prayers and Praise'. This is a regular title for a worship event which varies enormously from place to place—though singing has been a major feature of the 'Praise' part of the title, and the event is intended to advertise itself by this title as not being a communion service. The characteristic feature of such events is their freedom and open-ness; whilst the dangers to which they are most prone are the lack of scripture reading and serious ministry of the word, and the possibility of mere repetitiveness and even banality both in what is sung and in what is spontaneously celebrated. That is in no way to write down the principle, nor to disqualify it on account of poor instances of it in use. It is however to ascribe heavy responsibility to those who lead, and to assert the principle of critical reflection, even *when the presence and power of the Holy Spirit is discerned.* The fact that God uses or blesses an event is not an automatic canonization of all that is said and done.

These things said, I still believe that good teaching (not necessarily by monologue impact) should have a high priority in any planning of a second service of a Sunday.[1] The worst of all worlds is where a sung evensong is visibly declining towards extinction, and those who love its choral character are simply hanging on in the vain hope that people will one day return to *that.* The evidence is strong that this does not happen—and a new and fresh initiative is needed, even by the closing down of the existent service.

[1] One of the reasons why I have been ready to write much less about Sunday evenings in this booklet as compared with *Patterns of Sunday Worship* is that a much fuller and satisfying treatment of the subject is available in David Kennedy and David Mann, *Sunday Evening Worship* (Grove Worship Series no. 109, 1989), which I strongly recommend.

6. A PERSONAL DISCIPLESHIP

On page 8 above I have raised the question, in an historical context, as to *why* Victorian Anglicans went to Church. The same question hangs around today. Indeed although our church members may have a clearer sense of commitment to Jesus Christ than many of their predecessors, it is also true that the distractions from continually attending church week by week are much greater. Certainly the kind of determined attendance that marked the Victorians is rare even among responsible church members to-day.

So there is a question about our *seriousness* as individuals. There is a phrase around of a 'rule of life'.[1] Each individual Christian should be taking responsibility before God not only to build up in his or her own personal discipleship, but also to be *there* in a stated and known way in order to help build up others. The mere concern as to whether *I* shall benefit or not, or enjoy it or not, or feel better or not, is not sufficient basis for creating God's taskforce for mission for the present decade or the next millennium. No, we should reckon a duty to God and to our brothers and sisters in Christ, and *be* there. That is the key to the continuance and growth of the church of God.

APPENDIX: THE PLACE OF SUNDAY

It needs to be squarely faced in British church life that a distinctive Sunday is disappearing around us. This is a function not only of the recent collapse of legal restraints on shop and supermarket trading (which will certainly lead to some change in the law), but also of a fast spreading use of the day for sport, entertainment, commerce, industry, shift-working, and a host of other invasions. Whilst some Christians have resisted it all on quasi-sabbatarian grounds, others appear to have joined in it all on the grounds that there are no biblical or doctrinal boundaries of a legalistic sort. Hence the defensive campaign has been called no more than 'Keep Sunday Special', though clearly much Christian energy has gone into such campaigning.

If we acknowledge the truth of the inroads made by secularism into the 'traditional' Sunday, we have to ask ourselves whether corporate and worshipping Christianity should present itself as one of the following:

(a) a group which says you cannot belong to it if you cannot make its meetings;

(b) a group which is reasonably indifferent as to whether or not you can make its meetings;

(c) a group which is prepared to provide at least some 'main' worship events on other days of the week.

This choice takes us in vastly different directions when each possibility is applied to those seeking baptism for a child or wishing to be converted.

[1] See, for instance, Harold Miller, *Finding a Personal Rule of Life* (Grove Spirituality Series no. 8, 1984).